Single Mothers And Living For Christ

Tréasa Brown

Copyright © 2020 by **Tréasa Brown**

All rights reserved. No part of this publication may be reproduced by any means, graphics, electronic, or mechanical, including photocopying, recording, taping, or by any information storage retrieval system without the written permission of the publisher except in the case of brief quotations embodied in critical articles and reviews.

Tréasa Brown/Rejoice Essential Publishing

PO BOX 512

Effingham, SC 29541

www.republishing.org

Unless otherwise indicated, scripture is taken from the King James Version.

Single Mothers And Living For Christ/ Tréasa Brown

ISBN-13: 978-1-952312-31-1

Library of Congress Control Number: 2020914735

Dedication

    This book is dedicated to my Lord and Savior, Jesus Christ, who inspired me to write this book. I also would like to dedicate this book to my grandmother, Missionary Hazel Lee Hughes, who was the mother of 12 children. As well as all the anointed SINGLE mothers all around the globe. Be encouraged!

Contents

ACKNOWLEDGEMENTS..ix

PREFACE..xi

FOREWORD..xiv

CHAPTER 1:	My Testimony..........................1
CHAPTER 2:	The Past Is the Past...............................8
CHAPTER 3:	Enough is Enough..............................19
CHAPTER 4:	Desperation is the Issue.....................28
CHAPTER 5:	Healing Is A Must!..............................32
CHAPTER 6:	Where You Will Find Your Strength..40
CHAPTER 7:	You've Come Too Far to Go Back!........46
CHAPTER 8:	Know Who You Are In God!................55
CHAPTER 9:	You Are Not Who THEY Say You Are..62
CHAPTER 10:	The Anointing Is Attractive.................67

CHAPTER 11:	Investment (Encouragement to All Mothers)..76
ABOUT THE AUTHOR	84

Acknowledgements

Father, Son and Holy Ghost! Lord, You ALWAYS inspire me and have been my #1 encouragement. I would be lost without you!

To my three beautiful children, DeVontaé, Julissa, and Julius Steele, Mommy loves you. We're going to make it!

To my mother, Hazel Hughes-Choyce, who has under-girded, there's so much that I could say about you, but for now, I love you and thank you for ALL your prayers, you're the jewel in my life!

To my uncle Joe, you have always been like a father figure in my life. Thank you so much. I love you!

To my dad, Tommy Lee Brown, I love you and I'm praying for you!

To Daddy Choyce, thank you for all your support and prayers, we love you!

To my siblings, Caémeille Choyce, Tony and Tyler Brown, I love you all! We have been through a lot together, but God is going to get the GLORY out of our lives. It's our turn!

Finally, to all those that encouraged me during the process of writing this book, thank you so much! I'm sure you know who you are! Go easy on me, this is my FIRST! God bless you! Enjoy!

Preface

This book contains delicate chapters of my life and different obstacles that I faced. Often people see the anointing on our lives, but they don't know the process. We witness to others, but we often neglect our process and what happens in between struggle and victory. This is the part that needs to be heard! There's nothing wrong with being discreet, but where's the transparency?

In this book, not only am I transparent as a single mother, but I impart encouragement and Scripture to undergird my experience. The goal is to share my testimony with single mothers, or single women, in believing that they can learn through my story and reflect on their own current situations in life. My hope is that they will know their worth and value of who they are IN GOD! My prayer is that they will AVOID these same pitfalls and be the best woman of God they can be through Christ Jesus! This book is not to shine the light on all my flaws, but that people will know that we serve a MIGHTY God that causes TRANSFORMATION and GROWTH in us through in the process!

James 5:16 declares, "Confess your faults one to another, and pray one for another, that ye may be healed. The effectual fervent prayer of a righteous man availeth much." My process wasn't pretty, but the end result as the Lord continues to take me through WILL glorify HIM! I'm grateful for what the Lord has done in my life! I told the Lord that if He would give me a platform to testify to the young women, I would tell them what I've been through. Well, this was the way the Lord decided to do it even though I didn't see this coming.

He declared over my life that I was "Destined to be a writer, an Author..." I was amazed at the confirmation that came through other men and women of God who are divine connections in my life! "Single Mothers and Living For Christ," is meant to not only build up the single mothers, but encourage them in this walk with the Lord! We're NOT walking it out alone, but through HIM that gives us strength from day to day! I pray that you become empowered single mothers by the Word of God and that you embrace where you are in this season of your life!

Foreword

"Single Mothers and Living For Christ," by Tréasa Brown is an encouraging read for single moms and for those believing for their husband. I can relate to her story because I was a single mother for a few years before I remarried. The journey wasn't as easy as it appeared, but the Lord gave me strength and provided for my children and I. Single mothers don't have to compromise, but they can live for Jesus Christ. Tréasa Brown is transparent about her struggles and how she overcame them. She warns us about the enemy's pitfalls, so we don't make the same mistakes that many single mothers have previously. Her story is beautiful because she shares her salvation process and the sacrifices she made to become the woman of God that she is today. My husband and I have had the pleasure of interviewing Tréasa Brown on our podcast. I also co-authored another book with her, so I know that she is the real deal. She is serious about her walk with the Lord. She loves her children and is a great mother who has lots of knowledge to share. After you finish reading this book, make sure that you pass this copy along and plant a seed into another woman's life. She will thank you later. God bless.

—Kimberly Moses
Author of Becoming A Better You
Director at Rejoice Essential Magazine

CHAPTER 1

My Testimony

I was born and raised in Boulder, Colorado. My mother Hazel Hughes-Choyce, is the mother of 4 children: 2 boys and 2 girls. I'm the 3rd of the 4. I have a very unique conception testimony because my mother prayed for me and wrote my name on a Christmas stocking before I was conceived in the year of 1987, to be exact. That's faith! This was truly a miracle because the chances of conception were extremely low as my mother had previously tied her tubes and then reversed the process. With my mother's prayer in mind, I'm often reminded of Hannah. In bitterness of soul, Hannah made her petition to the Lord, that if He would give her a man child, she would give him, (Samuel) back to the Lord all the days of his life (See 1 Samuel 1:9-11). My mother just happened to pray for a girl! As a child, I was dedicated and given back to the Lord, as were my siblings. Hannah's prayer was answered! 1 Samuel 1:27 says, "For this child I prayed: and the Lord hath given me my petition which I asked of him." The Lord made conception possible, but my mother's pregnancy was very complicated. She began contracting early at the three month stage of pregnancy and her risks were severe. Anyone that knows about pregnancy knows that the chances of a baby's survival at three months are very slim.

Within this trimester of pregnancy, the baby is at the beginning stages of development. In fact, the most crucial stage of growth for the baby is considered to be within the last month of the 1st trimester. This caused my mother to be on bed rest for most of her pregnancy. I could've died in my mother's womb! I have heard before that prophets or prophetic people seem to have detrimental experiences at young ages or even later on in life. The enemy desires to take them out. All I can say is, this is a mark of letting you know that you are destined for greatness and the enemy wants to stop what God has already predestined, but he can't!

The blood of Jesus still works and covers us! When you have an anointing upon your life, there's a mandate and the assignment must be carried out. To God Be the Glory!!! I was formed in my mother's womb and was handcrafted by God! Jeremiah 1:8 declares, "Before I formed thee in the belly I knew thee; and before thou camest forth out of the womb I sanctified thee, and I ordained thee a prophet unto the nations." I can very much relate to this because the Lord has called me from my mother's womb.

The Bible also declares in Psalm 139:14, "I will praise thee; for I am fearfully and wonderfully made: marvelous are thy works; and that my soul knoweth right well." I'm a walking, talking miracle! I've had the enemy try to take me out on more than one occasion. There was a time I choked on a piece of pork chop steak like a baby and I remember thinking that I was going to be found dead by my children or family members in my kitchen. But the Lord spared my life and allowed the pieces that were stuck in my throat, to come out. After I gasped for air, I remember saying to myself, "I almost died...". There, I could've died in my sin!

That same day, I called my mother after the choking occurred and I remember her telling me that she almost got into a car accident on her way to work. The Lord covered her and it wound up being someone else in front of her. (Condolences to those persons) In addition, my sister almost got hit by a car, while walking to or from school, I was surprised. I almost felt like I was going to die while in labor with my daughter (my second child) while close to her delivery. I felt as though I was going to black out because there was some kind of shift taking place in my body. I remember the sound of the monitors in the hospital making a specific noise and the nurses coming to my aid while placing something in my IV. I remember feeling revived whenever they did this and it occurred more than once. I remember this quick urge of needing water and in my attempt to ask, they wouldn't let me and expressed that I could only have ice chips. Even then, the Lord was my keeper!

I've had the enemy speak to me while in my sister's room in an attempt to get some sleep one night. I heard him tell me, "I am going to take your life"! I also dreamed that a woman came up to me and told me the exact date of my death. While saying this, the woman showed no emotion and continued to walk down the hallway. As I prepared to tell my family with a heavy heart, I met my mother. In my mother's hand was a needle, the kind that doctors inject a patient with. As she injected me in my hand, I saw a drop of blood fall to the ground. That was the end of my dream. I was told not to receive the dream. I quickly rebuked the dream.

I often had thoughts about age 30. I would say to myself and others that it would be a blessing if I make it to that age. The enemy had placed fear and false thoughts in my mind. But through it all, the LORD has kept me and I'm STILL here even while writing this very book at 30! I believe that you, who are reading this book, have a testimony in your mouth and can attest to the Lord keeping you when you should've been gone. The Lord is yet the keeper of our soul and His divine protection is ever present.

The Lord spoke these prophetic words to me on August 9th 2018:
A book needs to be birthed out of you. ("Single Mothers and Living for Christ")...

You are going to get in touch with a book writer one day and write a book...

Be not afraid, daughter, to write the book when I give you release to do so...

You were destined to be a writer...An Author...

What I have locked up in your womb is priceless...

My Words are in there...

Don't be afraid, daughter, to step out on my Word...

Trust and believe I have spoken this to you...

Many need to know your testimony and what I have brought you from...

I have delivered you out of MANY things. And MANY need to know this...

Be not afraid of what I just told you...

These words for this book are locked up inside your belly...

But when I release you...You shall write and write and write...

Don't be afraid daughter, receive what I am telling you...

You will be released to do so...

Be not afraid, but trust what I have said unto thee...

I am your help Tréasa and this is for my Glory and my Glory only...

Believe...

The Lord continued to encourage me in that particular prophetic message. Wow! That was quite the download that He spoke over my life. I'm happy to say that those words have come to pass. Soon after, I met the book writer, Prophetess Kimberly Moses and I have written just as the Lord has spoken. That's profound! Sometimes we often think too small, but you can't put God inside of a box. We must learn to take Him at HIS Word and not our own. Numbers 23:19 declares, "God is not a man, that he should lie; neither the son of man that he should repent: hath he said, and shall he not do it? or hath he spoken, and shall he not make it good?" We serve too AWESOME of a God, to size Him up with a box. Our God is GREATER than that! Tell your testimony and don't be ashamed to shout it out to those you encounter, as the Holy Ghost leads you. Our testimony is to be shared with others and we are to let the Lord do the rest of what He will do as we open our mouth to tell it.

CHAPTER 2

The Past Is the Past

One thing that we must understand as single women or single mothers is that the past is the past! There are things that we can't go back and fix in past relationships, mistakes, or choices. This is why we must know who we are in Christ Jesus as the NEW creatures that He has created us to be in Him. 2 Corinthians 5:17 declares, "Therefore if any man be in Christ, he is a new creature: old things are passed away; behold, all things are become new." Paul also declares in Philippians 3:13-14, "Brethren, I count not myself to have apprehended: but this one thing I do, forgetting those things which are behind, and reaching forth unto those things which are before, I press toward the mark for the prize of the high calling of God in Christ Jesus."

We should no longer be stuck in our past. However, when we reach back there, it should be for transparency with another, in telling our story of how the Lord delivered us and brought us out! It's a reminder to give God praise for what He brought you out of, rejoice and give thanks unto Him! He didn't allow you to stay there. So often, we let the enemy hold our past over our heads and let others label us because of what they remember about us. We often keep ourselves there, instead of pressing forward. This, I'm sure can be draining mentally, emotionally, and spiritually. It can affect your growth.

Sometimes you need to remind them and yourself, that you are no longer in that category, neither do you have that mindset. People will literally attach your past with your present because that's all they remember or know about you. But you have to keep pressing and become who God said you are in Him. Don't become so stuck that you can't progress in the things of God, because of what someone has said, or labeled you as.

Also, don't look for validation from others, nor try to keep convincing them about your change. Live it and let Christ shine His light through you.

Believe me, when I say, people will notice the difference as you walk the walk. Some family members told me that they could see the change in my life and it inspired their growth because they knew my lifestyle before I was committed to God. To God Be the Glory! Their words encouraged me to keep going. 2 Corinthians 3:2 declares, "Ye are our epistle written in our hearts, known and read of all men." This says to me that you may be the only book that people will ever read, so make sure your content is in order. The transformation and growth happened over time as I walked with God. Jesus is real! He came into my life, cleaned me up and I'm still in a process and learning.

I can look back and see the tremendous transformation that the Lord made in my life. It's the best decision I've ever made and I thank Him for it. We are all striving to become the Woman of God that the Lord would like, together. My past does NOT define who I am today. At times, you have to encourage yourself in the Lord your God, as David did in 1 Samuel 30:6. It's easier said than done, but you WILL have to as a single mother, especially when no one else is there to assist you.

I will share something with you transparently. In 2014, I was hurt to the core when I put myself in a position with a young man that the Lord told me to get rid of. I was saved and filled with the Holy Ghost, seeking the Lord with all my heart. I hungered and thirst after the things of God. Then, I got distracted and picked up the very thing I was told to get rid of.

Sounds harsh, but the Lord knew what was best and He was trying to protect me. I was getting ready to move around this time and most of my things had been packed in boxes. Walking down my hallway, I came across a piece of paper with the young man's number written on it. Looking at his number, I thought this was a sign for me to get back in contact with him. I wanted to thank him for a message he sent me around my birthday to which I never responded.

After all, it had been two years. I wasn't sure what he was going to say, nor how he would react after two years, but I had a goal in mind. I was determined to call him. Sure enough, I called him and we had an interesting conversation. At that moment, all the right things were said and we were instantly reconnected. We began seeing each other and I began to become more distracted in my walk with the Lord. Not just that, but I even gave this man a special part of me, my body. My life was becoming a mess right before my eyes and I was stuck in a place of lust. I wanted to stop what I was doing, but I didn't know how to get free from it.

As single mothers, after years of celibacy, we can become tired of waiting and get caught up in the wrong situations. However, we must learn to hold out and be sold out to HOLINESS. 2 Thessalonians 3:13 declares, "But ye, brethren, be not weary in well doing." It always seems that when you're pushing and doing well, your testing time comes. Bottom line, I should've never compromised when it came to the Word of the Lord!

So now, there's a stronghold on my life that won't seem to break. Let me just say that you can be a man or woman of God, filled with the Holy Ghost and get caught up in a situation like this. Many are not transparent about their process that the Lord took them through. But someone needs to know that these struggle points are REAL!!! The flesh is real and, we, as single mothers have to ask the Lord to keep us chaste.

Chaste means abstaining from extramarital or from all sexual intercourse. Being celibate, abstinent, self-restrained and pure, (you get the picture). I was on fire for God, passionate about my walk with Jesus, but there was something that the Lord still needed to reveal in me concerning the condition of my heart. I needed maturity in this area of my life. Temperance!

This is why we must not move forward with unresolved issues in our heart, but rather ask the Lord to make us whole. Ask Him to heal and remove any remaining residue before proceeding forward. Single mothers, this is why we must develop intimacy with the Father! He had to break that stronghold off of my life. I know many might be thinking right now, "How can this be? How could you stoop that low as a woman of God?" But my process brought forth my purpose! I didn't go through this just for me, but the Lord allowed me to go through it for HIS GLORY to be a witness and testify that the Lord can deliver you out of it!

What I needed during this time of my life was deliverance and the Lord made it happen. My mother and I prayed at least twice around this difficult season of my life. And my breakthrough happened on the third prayer. I could trust her! She never spoke down on me, prayed with me and I remember her telling me so lovingly at one time, "You want to take the long way around." Can I keep being transparent? I knew what she meant and sadly at that time, I was willing to take that risk. I remember crying from the depths of my soul and was very godly sorry.

The phone calls and text messages begin to cease from the young man. As we know ladies, men can get quiet after they've gained what they wanted. I was hurt and irritable at the fact that there was no communication. But looking back at this situation, the Lord was at work! I went on my knees to pray and began to confess some things before the Lord. I remember telling Him how I was afraid of losing this individual. But there was something in me that caused me to ask the Lord to reveal everything and nevertheless, I prayed for the Lord's will to be done.

Being that I prayed from a sincere place, with tears streaming down my face, early the next morning, I received a very long text. The Lord had revealed EVERYTHING that I needed to know. I was shocked and hurt all at once, but it was for the best. After all, I prayed and asked the Lord to reveal and He heard my cry. I was hurt to the core of my being, but remember, the Lord told me plainly to "Get rid of Him," from the beginning.

Side note: When the Lord tells you to do something, just do it, but fully! I again prayed with my mother on the phone for the third time and I experienced the Lord's healing power like never before! This healing felt like medicine to my heart. The Lord was mending all the broken pieces right there on the spot! I was shocked at the level of healing I experienced. I thought if I got up off my couch or if I even moved, the comfort would go away or be lifted up off of me. I thought the pain would come back again, but not so! That's how good the healing felt at that moment and I was surprised because typically I was so used to the pain lingering.

I know MANY of you have been there and know what I'm talking about when I refer to the lingering pain!

Something that I remember from that prayer is the Lord letting me know that He knows what I want. He ministered to me about the very best. He wants me to have the very best?! After all I did and have done? I know some of you might be thinking, "Of course He wants you to have the very best!" However, some of you might be surprised at the defeating thoughts the enemy will bring to the mind. That's why we have to cast down every imagination and high thing that exalts itself above the knowledge of God (See 2 Corinthians 10:4-5).

Later, the test came back around. Only this time, I passed it! I humbled myself to tell the young man that I made a mistake. I conveyed that there are real men and women of God and that he didn't need to make it up to me. I needed to move on. The Lord is faithful and He is my healer! Single mothers, if you need healing, I declare and decree that your hour has come! The Lord wants to heal and make you whole in every area of your life, including myself. Be healed, be delivered and be set free from your current situation, because healing is a MUST!

Sometimes you feel that you have to settle and become desperate for love and relationships. We will talk about that in a later chapter. That word that the Lord spoke over me along with so many other encouraging words has kept me going for years. It has encouraged me to wait for His very best. Know that you are good enough! I know we hear this all the time, but really know you're worth and value, ladies. Don't settle for less or think you only fall in a certain category. Stop thinking that as a single mother, the Lord can't bless you with the very best.

There's a process in receiving the very best, but it's worth going through and worth waiting for! Desperation is not the answer and is only temporary. You want something that is meant to last. Jesus declares in Mark 10:9, "What therefore God hath joined together, let not man put asunder." The Lord has a divine plan for your life, but I'm discovering you have to be willing to go through a process, go through preparation and WAIT! It can't be rushed when it comes to what God has for you and His divine plan for your life.

With waiting comes self-discipline and it's not always easy in your season of waiting. Believe me, I know and you're not alone. You are a daughter of the Most High God and you should be in expectation for the very best. So you see, everyone has a past. Don't worry about it. All you need to do is REPENT, learn from it, and grow! Romans 3:23 declares, "For all have sinned, and come short of the glory of God." We all have come up short somewhere, that's why we need King Jesus, our Savior! Remember, the past is the past and the Lord has many GREAT things to perform in your life. The question is, do we believe? Are we willing to wait for it? Look forward to your future and leave the past where it belongs, behind you!

CHAPTER 3

Enough is Enough

There comes a time in your life where you must realize that enough is enough! What do I mean? You're tired of the cycle causing you to repeat the same undesired behaviors. You begin to outgrow your stages of immaturity. In Romans 7: 19-20, the Apostle Paul says, "For the good that I would do not: but the evil which I would not, that I do. Now if I do that I would not, it is no more I that do it, but sin that dwelleth in me." Do you ever find yourself doing something that you didn't intend to do? Or the very thing you were supposed to do, you wound up not doing it? This is exactly the point Paul is making here.

The Bible also declares in 1 Corinthians 13:11, "When I was a child, I spake as a child, I understood as a child, I thought as a child: but when I became a man, I put away childish things." When I was a young lady, I became pregnant with my first son during my senior year of high school. The Lord blessed me to graduate, but I was in a relationship that wasn't ordained by God. After staying in that relationship, I became pregnant with my daughter. Not acknowledging all the signs of warning that the Lord revealed along the way, even though I wasn't saved, I then became pregnant with my youngest son. Do you see the cycle?

I faced so many hardships in this relationship, and I made so many mistakes in staying in a place of sin. During this relationship, I remember having dreams of this young man cheating on me. I expressed the dream to him, not knowing what was going through his thoughts. I remember hearing the Lord speak to me one day and he told me something along the lines of, "What he really wants to tell you is that he's cheating on you." I was shocked at what I heard, but at that time, I didn't realize this was my prophetic gift at work. I thought the voice of the Lord was my own thoughts.

The Bible declares in Romans 11:29, "For the gifts and calling of God are without repentance." I thought I was making things up in my own mind, but looking back, it was the Lord speaking loud and clear, trying to catch my attention and warn me. This was during a time where the young man had something to tell me. He expressed that he might be moving to Florida. I was told how beautiful I was and he had tears in his eyes but he never expressed that he was cheating. It's a fact that I heard these words!

I carried on until one day there was a phone call for me as I got out of the shower. My mother answered the phone and said there was a young lady that wanted to speak with me. I picked up the phone and everything that I heard at that time, caused my heart to sink. I began to feel so many emotions all at once. My heart was racing!

The young lady expressed to me that she, too, was in a relationship with the man who was the father of my first born child at the time. I began to look in the crib where my newborn son was lying and I felt like breaking down to cry as she was speaking. I was shocked to my core, and shaking uncontrollably! Afterwards, I called to clarify with the source. Ladies, many of you have heard these words before. "I didn't cheat or "I never cheated on you," phrase. Most of us are familiar with this common saying.

The young lady and my boyfriend at the time got on a three-way call and he played the role of a devoted partner smoothly. I didn't know what to believe. What is a young mother to do? May I just note here this question is for all the ladies in general? When these red flags occur, believe every last one of them! Don't ignore the truth because you are afraid of it or don't want to acknowledge it. The end result: I was in fact cheated on.

Jesus declares in John 8:32, "And ye shall know the truth, and the truth shall make you free." See the truth for what it really is and if the Lord is trying to show you something, let Him show you. The Lord loves us enough to tell us the truth! I often ask the Lord for Him to tell me the truth, even if it hurts. It will hurt, but let Him reveal! It's for your making and it's working together for your good. Single mothers, I know you can think back to the time when you had a similar situation. Thank God for the exposure because it was to protect you and your family. You have to know when enough is enough.

As the years went on, the father of my three children and I ended up going our separate ways. The Lord already knew! By no means am I saying that he and his mother didn't step in and help with the kiddos. There were many times they did, but the burden ultimately fell on me in the long run. My mother used to tell me, "They are yours when they are nobody else's." You may have to read that a few times to get the full understanding.

The Lord had another plan for my life and that's what I had to understand. As a mother, I spent most of my time at home, raising my children and being a stay at home mom. It was challenging and still comes with many challenges along the way. However, I received help from my lovely sister and my loving mother. I'm grateful for them! Once in a blue moon in my early 20's, I would go out with my friends at the time. However, I tried to make the most of my time with my little ones.

There were times I didn't make healthy choices around this age and there were experiences I should've thought through. But the Lord never gave up on me and was longsuffering! Around age 23, I began to think, "There has to be more to life than this." The times that I went out to the club became less appealing to me and I began to think about what kind of example I would become for my children. Would I be snapping my fingers, dancing, and singing R&B music in front of them? What kind of example would that be? Living a loose life just wasn't the answer. Music is something that I thought about heavily. My story wasn't centered on drug addiction or alcoholism, because I never really enjoyed those things. I tried them and never really had a liking or taste for them, as much as others did. In fact, I had many reasons why I steered away from those things. They brought up thoughts about my own father and I didn't enjoy the company of those who consumed too much alcohol that couldn't handle it. My addiction was trying to figure out how I would give up all that "good music" that I enjoyed, specifically worldly R&B. I truly believe sex became another addiction of mine. I realized that before I gave my life to Christ, the Lord was already at work.

Though I had thought about music a lot, I was listening to Gospel more than I ever did over R&B, just before accepting salvation. When I got saved, over time, I didn't acknowledge it anymore. Before I knew it, the Lord took the desire away! On another note, I'm glad to say that I accepted salvation around the age of 23, in January of 2012 and was filled with the Holy Ghost on March 28th 2012. The Lord was really transforming my life and He began speaking prophetically to me even the more. I journaled what I believe He was saying to me along the way and I built an authentic relationship with Him from there.

I shared all that to say, know when enough is enough! As single mothers, we must understand that we need Jesus as our Lord and Savior. God must be the head of our lives! This is when we're truly in tune with the voice of God and have a sensitivity to the Spirit of God. The Lord was shifting my life right before my eyes.

To all my single mothers, know that you are an example before your children. Our children are paying close attention to what we do, more than we realize. They are taking notes whether we know it or not. The Bible declares in Proverbs 22:6, "Train up a child in the way he should go: and when he is old he will not depart from it." In order to train up a child in the way they should go, you need the Lord to lead and guide you as a parent. The Lord IS your covering!

In order for the leading and guiding to come in the right way, you also need the Holy Ghost. You can't live how you want to live. It's enough! You're bought with a price and are not your own. 1 Corinthians 6:19-20 declares, "What? Know ye not that your body is the temple of the Holy Ghost which is in you, which ye have of God, and ye are not your own? For ye are bought with a price: therefore glorify God in your body, and in your spirit which are God's."

Your choices can affect you and your family and there's more to consider than just you. Your steps need to be ordered by the Lord. Psalm 37:23 declares, "The steps of a good man ARE ordered by the Lord: and he delighteth in his way." Understand that you must acknowledge your missteps and want change. I wanted change in my life! Going down the path of destruction can be appealing to the flesh, but you'll realize the emptiness along the way and that your spirit man is yearning for the things of God.

Every mother needs guidance from the Almighty God. I don't care how good of a mother you claim to be or how many people tell you you're a great mother. There's always room for growth as a mother. Figure out what has been enough right now in your life and ask the Lord to change it. The cycle of routine is weighing you down, but the Lord is able to fix that too. Be willing to make adjustments and be honest with not just yourself, but honest and open with the true and living God! After being honest, mean it, let God change it and allow the Lord to create a new chapter in your life as a mother. Say goodbye to that chapter in your life because enough is enough!

CHAPTER 4

Desperation is the Issue

Desperation can be defined as the condition of being desperate, recklessness arising FROM despair. Despair is defined as to lose all hope or confidence. These two definitions seem to go hand in hand, but what shocked me the most was the other words that come with it. These include heartache, gloom, melancholy, anxiety, pain, agony, sorrow, grief, discomfort, despair, misery, fear, anguish, desolation, unhappiness, madness, defiance, distress, dejection and despondency. WOW!

Look at all the disadvantages connected to desperation. We break the spirit of desperation off of our lives when we plead the blood of Jesus and ask for the Lord to cover us in Jesus' name. We cancel the spirit of desperation and we claim victory over it in Jesus' name! When you find yourself in a place of desperation, you find yourself settling for less. I don't know about you, but to be honest, I have been in a place of desperation in my life when it came to relationships.

I, also, would find myself settling for less instead of striving and waiting for God's best. When you are desperate, you are basically in a position where there's no standard, there's no value and you've lost sight of your worth. The Bible declares in Matthew 7:6, "Give not that which is HOLY unto the dogs, neither cast ye your pearls before swine, lest they trample them under their feet, and turn again and rend you." With desperation, there's no vision, no ambition, and no goals. The Bible also declares to us in Habakkuk 2:2-3, "And the LORD answered me, and said, Write the vision, and make it plain upon tables, that he may run that readeth it. For the vision is yet for an appointed time, but at the end it shall speak, and not lie: though it tarry, WAIT for it; because it will surely come, it will not tarry." And Proverbs 29:18 declares, "Where there is NO VISION, the people perish."

As a single mother or just a single woman, we must have a vision and there must be a standard. There must be a goal in mind and we can't wallow in a place of desperation. We can take confidence in the Lord and trust that He wants the very best for His daughters. You see, ambition (aspiration, aim, purpose, dream, mission, and calling) is defined as a strong desire to do or to achieve something, typically requiring determination and hard work.

When there is ambition, you don't have time to be distracted and stagnant. You don't have time to be connected to people who are like a roadblock taking up space. You don't have time to wait on someone that was not destined nor ordained to be unified and become ONE with you. It's a waste of time! But you have to take a stand, be willing to wait and go through the process. It becomes tough in our waiting, but we have to be made, pushed, formed and we have to be birthed.

With this in mind, you can't be desperate and settle. But your mind has to be made up even in your waiting and with your tears, I'm determined! There may be a Word that the Lord has spoken over your life and it has not yet manifested, but still you await the manifestation. We can encourage one another to keep holding on because our redemption draws nigh. Luke 21:28, Jesus declares, "And when these things begin to come to pass, then look up, and lift up your heads; for your redemption draweth nigh." Hang in there woman of God! Hang in there sister in Christ!

The Lord is able to deliver you out of that place of desperation and bring you into a place that is full of His promises and the fullness of joy! Psalm 16:11 declares, "Thou wilt show me the path of life; in thy presence is fullness of joy; at thy right hand there are pleasures for evermore." All we have to do is hold on to that which He has already spoken. It's not easy, but it demands for us to come out of desperation and to wait patiently on what the Lord has in store for us!

CHAPTER 5

Healing Is A Must!

When I think of healing, I think of being revived, renewed, and strengthened. I think of being repaired and refreshed. Many of us need healing in many parts of our lives. We need God to do the unthinkable when it comes to His divine healing in our lives. TRANSFORMATION comes to mind.

So often we run away from the healing that the Lord has in store for us in certain areas because for some reason we are afraid of what's required of us. We don't want to give things up for it, which then keeps us in bondage and we try to bandage up the pain instead of receiving the proper cure for it. Bandaging is only temporary, but the real cure is everlasting! However, I assure you that if this healing is coming from God Almighty, you don't want to wait another minute! Be willing to give up whatever it takes to get your breakthrough when it comes to your healing.

Reach for it, embrace it, and receive it! It's not the will of God that we remain in a position of brokenness when it comes to us being whole in Him. He's able to heal the voided and empty places! Think of it this way, in order for something to function properly at its best, it must be fixable! When it comes to previous relationships, we as single Christian women or single Christian women with children, have to be aware of the dangers of not being FULLY healed and carrying baggage of hurt into what will soon be our Godly marriages, for the Glory of God. The Lord can't release something to us that we are not in position for.

A healing process must be set in position for the recipient that has been broken. From another point of view, some of us just want the healing, but we don't want the HEALER. We bring ourselves to a disadvantage that way. That's like the surgeon putting you to sleep without doing actual surgery! You won't receive the ultimate result at its fullest because you won't let the procedure take place.

In order for the procedure to be successful, it must be completed. What am I saying? God is not a partial God. He doesn't do things some of the ways, but He does things all the way. He does ALL things well! He wants you to have all of Him and He wants all of you! Think of a cut. When you receive a cut, the wound is open, blood is dripping and a stinging pain. But with the proper procedure to aid the cut, you notice that over time, the skin begins the healing process and before you know it, you begin to forget the pain and cut was even there. Jesus is the antidote to your pain! Take time to heal properly and let the Lord work HIS healing in you.

With burns, in order for the pain to be drawn out, sometimes HEAT is needed to draw out the pain of a burn. My mother taught us this as children. Whenever we had a particular burn, she would tell us to hold our burn over the stove. She would make us do it because the heat used, draws out the actual heat that is trapped within the wounded skin. It's a painful process in the present moment, but once done, the burn is soothed and brings relief over time.

During my own healing process, I have discovered what confession will do in your private prayer time with the Lord. As you confess your pain, hurt, worries, bothers, your brokenness welcomes God to step in and see about your current situation. Not only that, but He will begin to heal what you've expressed Him. How would you know that the Lord is a healer, without experiencing it firsthand? The Lord does know all, but He wants us to communicate it with Him, so that we might know Him for ourselves.

It's great to hear the testimonies of the Saints of God, but how about having your own testimony? Nobody can tell it like you can! The Bible declares in James 5:17, "CONFESS your faults one to another, and pray one for another, that ye may be healed. The effectual fervent prayer of a righteous man availeth much." Not only is it great to go directly to the Lord, but also with a trusted man or woman of God that you know is walking in the righteousness of God. Have them pray with you, touch and agree.

There's a blessing in agreeing with someone for your current situation. Jesus declared in Matthew 18:20, "For where two or three are gathered together in my name, there am I in the midst of them." I shared with you in chapter 2, my experience of the healing power of God, as my mother prayed for me. As she prayed, the burden was lifted and the Lord was right there in the midst. He was healing my heart! I have been healed so many times! Even in my physical body, which I will also share.

The Lord is the Master healer who is able to heal the mind, body, soul and spirit. He can heal places that man cannot. The Lord healed my body of abnormal cells, which were known as HPV precancerous cells in my cervix. I endured so much as a young mother in my singleness. After receiving a Pap test sometime before my son was born, that's when the chaos began.

On March 15th, 2006, I received a letter that my PAP was slightly abnormal and that I would have to be retested. I was told in a letter that the test showed some atypical cells and tested positive for HPV. I needed a colposcopy, which is similar to a regular Pap test. I was also told the importance of having this procedure done because if untreated, it could lead to cervical cancer. I remember crying, being fearful and making a vow to the Lord. I told the Lord that if He got me out of this, I wouldn't do it anymore. My mother took the letter at that time, stuck it in her Bible and prayed for me as well. She wanted it to be her and pleaded to the Lord for it not to be me. She was willing to stand in my stead. Wow!

What an intercessor, what a mother! But I didn't keep that promise along the way. I stayed in a place of fornication during a certain time period. Anyhow, I received that abnormal PAP and sometime after 2007, I had a biopsy. This allows the doctor to take a closer look at the abnormal cells in the woman's cervix. More specifically, a biopsy is defined as an examination of tissue removed from a living body to discover the presence, cause, or extent of a disease.

Once the doctor examined the abnormal cells the next step was to do what they call a LEEP procedure, which is a shaving of the abnormal cells with a laser. (My goodness was it painful!) Do you know what it's like to be in and out of the doctor's office on a constant basis? This resulted in my disobedience, my own rebellion. Let me just say ladies, your life must be prioritized over pleasure. It's not worth it!

There are things that the Lord didn't intend for us to go through, but because we picked it, there was a great price and consequence attached to what we chose. I'm pleased to share this testimony that on August 18th of 2019, I received a letter stating: "Dear Tréasa Brown: We are pleased to let you know that your recent PAP test and HPV test are normal. This means that you do not need co-testing for PAP and HPV for 3 to 5 years". Hallelujah! This is certainly to be celebrated!

For so many years, because of the LEEP procedure that took place, I had to do PAP testing EVERY YEAR even if I was not sexually active. So from the year of the LEEP to 2019, it was mandatory. You could say I was like the woman with the issue of blood. I praise God that even before this letter was sent out, ALL PAPS after that procedure came back normal every year. Even the blood work that was done was said to be beautiful! Some may say, "Well you got the procedure, so that was what helped the situation."

However, I beg to differ. So many procedures can go wrong and people can still face a life threatening situation because a procedure has failed. If the Lord's hand is not in it, ANYTHING can go wrong and I do mean ANYTHING! This is a good spot for me to give God the GLORY! Thank You, JESUS! If it had not been for Him, I would not be healed today. This testimony has been seen by many on my YouTube channel and I have received so MANY positive responses. Many have asked for prayer, some have been encouraged, some have shared their brief story with me, and MANY have celebrated my healing! God gets the Glory and I praise Him that I made it out alright. I don't care what area you may need your healing in. GOD IS ABLE!

CHAPTER 6

Where You Will Find Your Strength

So many people have complimented me on the quality of my motherhood, my strength and the way I've raised my three children. They encourage me to keep doing what I'm doing. To God Be the Glory. All the credit belongs to God because without HIM, I can do nothing (See John 15:5)! Psalm 73:26 declares, "My flesh and my heart FAILETH: but God is the STRENGTH of my heart, and my portion forever." Or how about Psalm 40:31, "But they that wait upon the LORD shall renew their STRENGTH; they shall mount up with wings as eagles; they shall RUN and NOT be weary; and they shall walk, and NOT faint."

I appreciate the encouraging words and acknowledgment, but many don't see behind the scenes when mothers are at their lowest. However, without the FOUNDATION of the Word of God, I would've been so messy and very lost. Yet, the Lord is STILL perfecting some parts of me and pruning what is not like Him. Mommy needs work! Whether we like to admit it or not, to the public, we appear one way, while behind closed doors, there's yet another story. They don't see all your flaws and missteps.

Again, there's always room for growth as a mother, in so many different areas. It's true! When the Lord begins to go into the deep parts of your heart and reveal, He will begin to pull and weed out things that you didn't realize were there. This is not just as His daughter, but as the mother as well. God prunes and it is painful but we must learn to smile through our discomfort. When I say that my smile is TRULY a gift from God, it is, but I hurt too! Many have complimented this smile that God gave me and encouraged me to keep doing so. However,

MANY misunderstand its sincerity. Though I hurt, it's sincere. I'm going somewhere here.

Many of us single Christian mothers smile and walk around as if we have an 'S' on our chest representing super mom. But the flesh side of mommy is hurting, tired, worn out, needy, frustrated and so many other things that come with the title of a mom! I've hidden MANY things behind my smile, though I meant well. However, there comes a time as single mothers, we must humble ourselves and recognize the real source of our strength. I have MANY weak moments and have made MANY mistakes in parenthood. Haven't we all?

Let me say this, "It's ok to cry, to be angry, and sin not, according to Ephesians 4:26." It's ok to need some space and want time to yourself. It's all right when you're fed up with particular situations that happen in the home. We all have meltdowns, but here's the key! Go before the Lord, pour out your heart and soul to Him in prayer and confess what you will before Him.

In fact, tell Him EVERYTHING! You will find much strength in that particular prayer. Jesus had a moment right before His betrayal and arrest. Before enduring the cross, in Matthew 26:39 it declares, "And he went a little further, and fell on his face, and prayed, saying, O my Father, if it be possible, let this cup pass from me: nevertheless not as I will, but as thou wilt." Jesus had to pray to the Father! Oftentimes throughout the Bible, we read about Him turning aside to go pray ALONE.

Sometimes as single mothers, we can become too prideful but we have to be careful. What do you mean woman of God? We don't allow others to step in and give us a hand up because we're so used to doing everything on our own. The Lord sends true help and we reject it! We get so stuck in our routine that we aren't open for change- I'm talking about me. We have to be careful of 'my way or the highway' attitude. There is nothing wrong with a strong woman, who has goals and a standard. But have you ever wondered why we're so out of strength and worn down? It's because we often try to bear the tasks on our own and this can bring on spiritual warfare. There needs to be a release!

We don't always do everything right. We don't always correct our children the right way. In fact, we don't always have the perfect plan with our ducks in a row. There's a remedy for our struggles. The sweet name of JESUS! I love the way it's put in Psalm 121:1-2 which declares, "I will lift up mine eyes unto the hills, from whence cometh my help. My help cometh from the LORD, which made heaven and earth." Or Psalm 46:1, "God IS our REFUGE and STRENGTH, a very PRESENT help in trouble."

Learning to lean on Jesus and depending on Him to be everything is easier said than done. But it comes with RELATIONSHIP, growing and trusting in Him. I can attest to Him being my strength SO MANY TIMES. And now of course, I realize it's been Him ALL the time!

So many times, I was tired and wanted to throw in the towel and say, "Forget it!" But coming into the presence of the Lord, crying out to Him on my face, and hearing Him speak such encouraging words to me was the ONLY source of strength for me. Psalm 84:2 declares, "My soul longeth, yea, even fainteth for the courts of the LORD: my heart and my flesh crieth out for the living God. He is my ANCHOR! His words are more precious than fine gold. His Word brings life, because He IS the life!"

The Lord IS your STRENGTH! No matter what you're going through, depend on GOD to be everything you need. As I say this to others, I'm saying it to myself! Literally, it's a word of strength to me right now, due to my current situation! No one can give you the strength but God. Because of Him, you're able to do what you do. It is by God that you endure the things you've endured, put up with the things you've put up with and lived through what you've managed to live through! No matter how hard you work, plan, or feel like you've sacrificed, it's nobody BUT God! You'll ALWAYS find your source of strength IN HIM. Let it work for you!

CHAPTER 7

You've Come Too Far to Go Back!

You know, you may not be where you want to be right now, but you're certainly further than you once were. Think about it... If the Lord didn't deliver you, it could've been much worse. But look at you now, blossoming into the woman of God that the Lord has called you to be! Some of you that may be reading this book may say, "I have not made it there yet." But you have gotten to the point of reading this book right now is a stepping stone and a checkpoint! Not because this is my book, but because the Lord has purposed for you to read it!

Taking action and a step of faith can lead to MANY great things when it's all in the will of God. Just think about Peter. He took a risk to walk out on the water to Jesus, not knowing about the boisterous wind, but the Lord saved him! His faith had to be activated to a certain extent in order for him to START to walk towards Jesus on the water. Matthew 14:13 says, "And immediately Jesus stretched forth his hand, and caught him, and said unto him, O thou of little faith, wherefore didst thou doubt?" He had little faith and he doubted, but he tried. There was a lesson in him stepping out and there was something for Him to learn.

By no means am I saying that we should doubt the Lord and not grow in our faith. Without faith, it is impossible to please Him and there's always room for growth! Hebrews 11:6 declares, "But without faith it is impossible to please him: for he that cometh to God must believe that he is, and that he is a rewarder of them that diligently seek him." The Bible also declares in James 1:8, "A double minded man is unstable in all his ways."

What I am saying is that Peter took a risk and stepped out. He had a starting point!

So often, we focus on Peter taking his eyes off of Jesus, being afraid and beginning to sink because he saw the wind boisterous (See Matthew 14:30). Yes, there's a point to that. But look at Peter's WILLINGNESS to come to Jesus. Reading this book may be out of some of you ladies' comfort zone, but I assure you and would like to declare and decree over your life, that God is doing a new thing in you as you read this book! Matthew 14:28-29 declares, "And Peter answered him and said, Lord, if it be thou, bid me come unto thee on the water. And he said, Come. And when Peter was come down out of the ship, he walked on the water, to go to Jesus." Trying was better than not trying at all. It was a beginning point, a place of learning, and an ACT of faith!

When Jesus mentioned Peter's little faith, it indicated that growth in his faith needed to take place, wouldn't you say? His faith wasn't where it needed to be, but he had some. He was being stretched beyond the norm! We all have regrets from our past, but the question is, what are you going to do NOW, TODAY, at this very moment to move forward? Are you willing to be stretched as well? Or will you go back?

We are able to CHOOSE by the grace of God, what we want to change and what decisions we will make. We ought to want the change and our decisions to be based on the Lord's will. If I may encourage you right here, single mothers, keep pressing to your destiny, and towards who the Lord has called you to be in Him. If you aren't there yet, I encourage you to SEEK the Lord, get to know Jesus for yourself. Connect with someone who knows Him and can tell you all about Him. Or, pray and ask the Lord to REVEAL Himself to you and give you DIVINE CONNECTIONS in this season of your life. And when you ask Him, expect the results and the answer to what you've asked of Him.

Be like Peter and step out, try, and learn. Be stretched beyond YOUR OWN ability and let Jesus do what He alone does best because you can't do it on your own. Our God IS an awesome God and He can be trusted with your life in His hands. HE created you! I know I'm not the only one who has experienced old things trying to come back to the surface. The reality in life is that

MANY old things will try to come back and manifest, but you have the POWER to make a decision and change it.

Something powerful that the Lord gave us when He created us was our tongue. There's POWER in that tongue of yours, according to Proverbs 18:21, which declares, "Death and life are IN the power of the tongue: and they that love it shall eat the fruit thereof". You can speak to a thing and it shall be so, in Jesus' name! We have to realize the POWER and AUTHORITY that the Lord gave us when we open our mouth to speak. What are you saying woman of God? You can speak to the old things that try to come back and they shall be no more! Don't entertain it, move forward!

You don't have to revert back, because you've come too far! Some things are better left alone, on the shelf, where you once left it! Old relationships, old situations, old habits, old ways don't have to take place in your life. Neither do you have to let it rule over you. You have the POWER over it, with the Holy Ghost on the inside! If you don't have the Spirit of God on the inside of you, then maybe it's time you start seeking for Him and ask the Lord to fill you. It's a gift to all BELIEVERS who ask for it!

Something I've learned while being a single Christian mother is not to return to something that you know won't benefit you with where the Lord is taking you. Where you're going, everything can't come with. I say this with humility, but I'm serious. Where the Lord wants to take many of us, we don't have time to toil with the old, but we have to strive for the new. Don't go back! The Bible declares in Proverbs 26:11, "As a dog returneth to his vomit, so a fool returneth to his folly." What is folly? Folly is described as the lack of good sense, foolishness, stupidity and silliness.

You're one step closer to getting your breakthrough! One step closer to working towards something new. You will be closer to meeting your next goal, because you've come too far. While you're out there, go ALL THE WAY! We can learn from Lot's wife, when she turned into a pillar of salt, because she disobeyed the instructions that the Lord gave, in not looking back. In this chapter, the two angels of the Lord came to destroy the city of Sodom and Gomorrah. Specific INSTRUCTIONS were given to Lot concerning him and his family and how they were to escape.

Genesis 19:17 declares, "And it came to pass, when they (the angels) had brought them forth abroad, that he said, Escape for THY LIFE: LOOK NOT BEHIND THEE, neither stay thou in all the plain; escape to the mountain, lest thou be consumed." Those were specific instructions given by the Lord. However, something very profound happens in verse 24-26. Those verses declare, "Then the Lord rained upon Sodom and upon Gomorrah brimstone and fire from the Lord out of heaven; And he overthrew those cities, and all the plain, and all the inhabitants of the cities, and that which is good upon the ground." (Here it is) But his wife LOOKED BACK FROM BEHIND HIM, and she BECAME a pillar of salt. Too busy looking back at what was behind her, Lot's wife never made it to see what was before her.

Just look at Moses and a majority of the children of Israel. MANY DIED in the wilderness and never entered into the Promised Land. Moses only got to look, but didn't go over either! The Bible declares in Deuteronomy 34:1-5, "And Moses went up from the plains of Moab unto the mountain of Nebo, to the top of Pisgah, that is over against Jericho. And the Lord SHEWED him all the land of Gilead, unto Dan, And all Naphtali, and the Land of Ephraim, and Manasseh, and all the land of Judah unto the utmost sea, And the south, and the plain of the valley of Jericho, the city of palm trees, unto Zoar. And the LORD said unto him, This is the land which I sware unto Abraham, unto Isaac, and unto Jacob, saying, I will give it unto thy seed: I have caused thee to SEE it with thine eyes, but thou shalt NOT go over thither. So Moses the servant of the Lord died there in the land of Moab according to the word of the Lord."

How can we apply this for today? Don't die in your moment of progression. Don't die before you get to the promises of God. I'm not talking literally, but in a sense of, don't give up, don't get distracted, don't throw in the towel, don't have a K.O.! Push, persevere, get your tenacity back, get your drive back, get your motivation back and let the old things go!

Go further, deeper, and higher with the help of the Lord! Those old things are like baggage, dead weight and road blocks that hold you back from your promise. As I say this to you, I'm saying this to myself as I'm writing. I've cried so many tears as a young mother. I had many frustrations, many nights where I felt like I was alone, had people turn their back on me, backbite, hurt me, lie on me, use me and miss-treat me.

I'm moving forward! I have no desire to go back and revisit my past. I've left it with God. He's been my #1 encourager and has matured me in many areas from my past. He's the Author and the Finisher of my faith, according to Hebrews 12:2. I hope this chapter has encouraged you! Go woman of God, mom, single lady in Christ! You can do it, you've come too far. PROCEED!

CHAPTER 8

Know Who You Are In God!

Oftentimes, we're too busy trying to find our identity in the wrong things. We're looking to find our identity in our jobs, relationships, spouses for those who are married and much more. Your identity is hidden in Christ Jesus! Until you get to know Him, you will NEVER know who you truly are because you will be too busy looking in the wrong places. You may find what you're good at or gifted at in the world, but what about your true identity and your gifts for the Kingdom of God? Your God-given assignments?

Who are you in the Spirit? Because your Spirit Man is the real authentic you! Flesh is real, but our Spirit Man is more real than we know it to be! We are spiritual beings, and here's the reason. Genesis 1:27 declares, "So God created man in his OWN image, in the image OF GOD created he him; male and female created he them. So if we are created in GOD'S OWN IMAGE, then we are Spirit. Still not convinced?" John 4:24 declares, "God IS a Spirit: and they that worship him MUST worship him IN SPIRIT and IN TRUTH." The truth is: we are not our own and belong to God. 1 Corinthians 6:19 and 20 also declares, "What? know ye not that your body is the temple of the Holy Ghost which is in you, which ye have of God, and ye are not your own? For ye were bought with a price: therefore glorify God in your body, and in your SPIRIT, which are God's."

I encourage you single mothers to get to know the real you, through Jesus Christ our Lord. Some of you may ask," How do I find my identity in Christ?" The answer is through your relationship with Christ. As you walk and talk with the Lord to build the relationship, it's through fasting, prayer and reading God's Word that you will become closer and learn more about who you are in Him. Seek His face through the above listed practices. As you get into the presence of God, you will build intimacy with Him. As you learn the voice of God through your private time of prayer with Him, He will begin to tell you things about yourself.

I'll never forget when I was a new babe in Christ. He would speak to me so sweetly. I positioned myself much in prayer and would journal and hear the voice of God. He would reveal to me my gifts that He has placed on the inside of me and later, these gifts would get confirmed by others. There's no way that those that confirmed what the Lord had already spoken to me would know what I had written down, neither what He told me in private. The God that I serve is real and it was always a blessing to receive confirmation!

Let's look at a detailed example in my life. In the beginning of my walk, I wanted to know my purpose. I wanted to know what the Lord called me to be in Him. I remember gravitating to the prophetic. Now keep in mind that I knew nothing about the prophetic. I understood very little about prophets and even though I was 'born and raised' in the church, and knew the books of the Bible as a little girl, I never discovered that many of those books were the names of various prophets. Isn't that something? Many of you may say, "Tréasa that's strange that you didn't know that certain books of the Bible were prophets." But I tell you the truth. I didn't know until I became an adult and matured in the Word.

One day as I was journaling, the Lord began to speak to me and told me that I was a prophet. I couldn't believe what I heard and I often went through MANY seasons of doubt, in so much that I tried to get validation from people. I was looking for confirmation from man, rather than trusting in God and letting what He said be enough. He definitely corrected me and let me know He validates who I am. One day when I sat down with my children and read the Word of God with them, the Lord began to use my daughter at that time to tell me that I was a prophet.

I remember her saying these few words, "Mommy, but you are a prophet"...she began to tell me in a few words of WHY and I was shocked! He would use my brother to tell me, "You are the Lord's prophetess."...I had no idea that the Lord was using people that were closest to me to catch my attention. My mother would often encourage the same. A young prophet at the time by the name of Aldi Essandjo was in Denver, Colorado, doing a conference called, "Expect the Unexpected." I attended the conference and told myself that I would not look for a word to confirm my identity. However, I still received a prophecy over my life, and after his service, the Prophet spoke to me personally and said, "There's a prophetess down on the inside of you." I was so excited that night!

All I remember is being sucked in towards studying the prophetic. I bought my first book by Jennifer LeClaire called, "The Making of a Prophet," not really knowing if this was something that I was called to. I remember thinking, "What if I'm not a prophet?" But little did I know God was the orchestrator of it all! I remember hearing a song called "Like Jeremiah," as I began to weep, not realizing that my spirit man was connecting with who the Lord was calling me to be. It wasn't until I stopped looking for confirmation through man, that the Lord began to affirm me through others. He confirmed it, just like He said he would!

Then a test arose! The Lord began to speak to me and forewarned me of a test that was going to come. I was tested concerning who He called me to be. I had bonded with a woman of God and was thinking that I would be able to connect with her and get information and pointers on being a prophetess. We were certainly on the same page when we first spoke, but later, that all changed and shifted. Some months went by before we got a chance to connect with one another. When we spoke, I was shocked to my core. By the time I got off the phone, I felt as though my identity was stripped away from me. I began to doubt who I was in the Lord and I was crying, thinking to myself, all this fasting, praying and seeking the Lord's face and I've got to start all over?

The Lord, shortly after that phone call, began to speak to me and encouraged me. This was profound to me because I was thinking, "This is a woman of God that told me this." I reached out to my mother. She was one who that I knew would undergird and pray for me. As she prayed and encouraged me, one simple thing she said was, "You can't receive everything from everybody!" She was absolutely right. As she prayed and ministered to me, it's like she was building me back up in the spirit. Spiritual construction! It took reassurance along the way and I began to get stronger again. My Aunt, Christine, later ministered to me and the Lord spoke a mighty encouraging word of how I grew from the incident. Hallelujah!

Can I encourage some single mothers' right here? Believe what the Lord has spoken over your life! Be who HE SAYS you are and don't conform to what man has limited you to. Own who you are in Christ! Wear it, embrace it, guard your anointing and fight for it. Believe the report of the Lord! The Scripture that comes to mind particularly is 2 Peter 1:10 which declares, "Wherefore the rather, brethren, give diligence to make your calling and election sure: for if you do these things, ye shall never fall. Be confident in Christ Jesus!" I leave you with this Scripture, Romans 8:31, "What shall we say to these things? If God be for us, who can be against us?" Know who's backing you up and recognize who YOU ARE in God, mama!

CHAPTER 9

You Are Not Who THEY Say You Are

When we run into people from our past, they can only think of what they last remember about us. They will reminisce on those moments and cause you to think back. It's ok to reflect upon where the Lord has brought you from because we never want to forget our journey, story or testimony. However, we don't want our mentality to keep us in those places. As many have declared, "ELEVATE your thinking!"

When you begin to meet your past face to face, it's time to introduce your present! Approach it as an opportunity to testify to that person about where the Lord has taken you from. When you look at the Apostle Paul, in Acts chapter 9, he encountered Jesus on his way to Damascus. He persecuted the church, but after that encounter, Saul's name changed to Paul and he was never the same again. Did you catch that? He experienced such a change that the Apostle received a new name. Glory to God! Won't the Lord do it for you? He will not only change your name, but your reputation, both in the natural and spiritual!

Paul gets converted and is now a follower of Jesus Christ. This happens after Ananias, gets word from Jesus to "go into a street which is called Straight, and enquire in the house of Judas for one called Saul, of Tarsus:....(See Acts 9:11). He lays his hands on Saul that he may receive his sight and is filled with the Holy Ghost. Here's the interesting part. The Bible declares in Acts 9:20, "And straightway he preached Christ in the synagogues, that he is the son of God!" That's an immediate transformation in which Paul was equipped and ready for the work of the Lord! Specifically chosen by Jesus for such a task, even though he had a past.

Going further into the Scripture, Acts 9:26-27 declares, "And when Saul was come to Jerusalem, he assayed to join himself to the disciples: but they were all afraid of him, and believed NOT that he was a disciple. But Barnabas took him, and brought him to the apostles, and declared unto them how he had seen the Lord in the way, and that he had spoken to him, and how he had preached boldly at Damascus in the name of Jesus." What are you saying woman of God? There are many that won't believe the change that you have encountered because they simply can't get past who you once were. You won't have to defend yourself! As we hit on before, let your lifestyle and the light that shines through you be enough. Think of it as, the way I live is the line of demarcation from my past. I'm in a relationship with the Father, Son and Holy Ghost and no one can take that away from me.

Even Paul was identified by others as what he was known for and not what/who he became. Don't respond to the titles of who you once were. Only respond to who the Lord has called you to be. When you begin to put emphasis on your past, you magnify the old man, instead of highlighting the new man in Christ Jesus. Never feel that you have to prove anything to anyone, just live your life for Christ and let the Lord do the validating.

Single mothers are often labeled as ones who failed in a relationship or marriage, a mother who had a child/children out of wedlock, or someone who's desperate for love. Remember, your title goes beyond "Mommy"! You're called to do more than just bare children. You've got more to offer than just being a housewife, clean house, work a job and cook meals. Whatever you've been labeled as by others that was not of God, eject it from your spirit man and grab ahold of how the Father sees you in HIS eyes. You're beautiful, strong, and fearfully are wonderfully made! You're the apple of the Father's eye. I declare and decree that we are unique in Jesus' name and that the Lord has given us a new name, as His daughters in Christ Jesus! Speak it over yourself and walk in it P31 woman. (For those that have never heard this term, a P31 woman, it's a Proverbs 31 woman, please read it).

Many would like to remember me for a lot of things concerning my past, but I will no longer carry those labels around with me into my future. Colossians 3:10 declares, "And have put on the new man, which is renewed in knowledge after the image of him that created him." Jesus has changed my name both in the natural and spiritual, as we have discussed earlier with Paul. My old record is behind me and my reputation has a new clean slate. My identity is hidden with Christ. Colossians 3:3 declares, "For ye are dead, and your life is hid with Christ in God."

My flesh needs to be crucified daily, so that I don't fulfill the lust of the flesh. Galatians 5:24 declares, "And they that are Christ's have crucified the flesh with the affections and lusts." Push past your flesh by letting prayer and fasting be your portion. The Lord encouraged me this year and simply said to me, "Be uniquely you daughter"... As simple as it was, I was very encouraged by it! We need those reminders as we're moving forward in life. For the sake of being hurt by others or thinking we need the approval of another. God is raising some profound women like we have seen in the Bible. I declare that WE are those women of today! Remember, you're not who they say you are, but rather it's what you respond to!

CHAPTER 10

The Anointing Is Attractive

Anointing is defined as: to smear or rub with oil; to consecrate, sanctify, bless, ordain or hollow. In addition, attraction can be defined as pleasing, appealing, inviting, interesting or alluring. When you look in the Bible, you will find many that were anointed for a specific task for the glory and honor of God. We often look at Saul from one main standpoint, but he was anointed as king, though he disobeyed God. 1 Samuel 10:1 declares, "Then Samuel took a vial of oil, and poured it upon his head, and kissed him, and said, Is it not because the LORD hath anointed thee to be captain over his inheritance? David was next in line to be anointed king." 1 Samuel 16:13 also declares, "Then Samuel took the horn of oil, and anointed him in the midst of his brethren: and the Spirit of the LORD came upon David from that day forward. So Samuel rose up, and went to Ramah."

Others in the Bible may not have specifically been anointed with oil, but were still anointed and chosen by God. For example Apostle Paul, in Acts 9:15-16 it says, "But the Lord said unto him, (Ananias) Go thy way: for he is a chosen vessel unto me, to bear my name before the Gentiles, and kings, and the children of Israel: For I will shew him how great things he must suffer for my name's sake." Continuing down to Acts 9:17-18, it declares, "And Ananias went his way and entered into the house: and putting his hands on him said, Brother Saul, the Lord, even Jesus, that appeared unto thee in the way as thou camest, hath sent me, that thou mightiest receive thy sight, and be filled with the Holy Ghost. And immediately there fell from his eyes as it had been scales: and he received sight forthwith, and arose, and was baptized." Paul was anointed for a particular assignment!

Jesus, being our ultimate example, did the will of the Father. He was the chosen one, the Messiah, before the foundation of the world. The one spoken of to Mary that He would be the Son of the highest, EMMANUEL. Our Lord and King! Jesus declared in Luke 4:18-19, "The Spirit of the Lord is upon me, because he hath ANOINTED me to preach the gospel to the poor; he hath sent me to heal the brokenhearted, to preach deliverance to the captives, and recovering of sight to the blind, to set at liberty them that are bruised, To preach the acceptable year of the Lord." What am I saying here? There are many single mothers like myself that are anointed. The anointing of the Lord is upon your life and the Lord has chosen you for such a time as this. God's almighty hand is heavy upon your life, not just to be mommy, but to walk in His power and into great destiny!

What do I mean by stating that the anointing is attractive? It can draw great attention both in the natural and spiritual. For example, there are times I think to myself, why do I attract particular men? If I can be transparent, there are specific men that I've been approached by in times past that seem to have the wrong motives, but so much potential. Or, they're just not of interest to me in the beginning, but somehow in the long run, they manage to capture my attention. I have thought to myself, how did I get in this situation, or what was I thinking? The anointing seems to attract the unusual, but you must discern what you are attracting!

The Bible declares in 2 Corinthians 11:14, "And no marvel: for Satan himself is transformed into an angel of light." In Acts 16:16-18, we see that Paul and Silas had an encounter with a damsel with a spirit of divination, while on the journey preaching the gospel. It declares, "And it came to pass, as we went to prayer, a certain damsel possessed with a spirit of divination met us, which brought her masters much gain by soothsaying: The same followed Paul and us, and cried, saying, These men are the servants of the most high God, which shew unto us the way of salvation. And this did she many days. But Paul, being grieved, turned and said to the spirit, I command thee in the name of Jesus Christ to come out of her. And he came out the same hour." The anointing attracts warfare and demonic spirits who have demonic assignments.

As a woman of God, I've noticed the enemy will send distractions, hindrances, and counterfeits that will derail you and reroute you, from your assignment. Why? Simply, because the anointing attracts! They'll try to kill your destiny. We have to learn how to war in the spirit during prayer and guard our anointing! Because the Lord has chosen and anointed you and I for a particular assignment, the enemy will do all he can to strip you of your anointing.

1 Samuel 16:14 declares, "But the Spirit of the LORD departed from Saul, and an evil spirit from the LORD troubled him. And Saul's servants said unto him, Behold now, an evil spirit from God troubleth thee." There's too much at risk when it comes to the oil or the anointing that's upon your life. That's why you have to be careful of people who try to lure you away from the things of God and want you to follow after the flesh. Romans 8:8 declares, "So then they that are in the flesh CANNOT please God." Verse 13-14 says, "For if ye live after the flesh, ye shall DIE: But if ye through the Spirit do mortify the deeds of the body, ye shall live. For as many as are led by the Spirit of God, they are the sons of God."

A woman of God caused me to realize that some people are simply attracted to the anointing that's upon my life, rather than my beauty. It's a spiritual thing! I couldn't agree more and find this to be true in my life. Have you ever heard someone tell you, they just don't know what it is about you? Or, how they just can't figure out what attracts them to you? All my life, I've been told, "You're so different," by different men. They often find it shocking of just HOW different I am from other young ladies. Could it be that it's the anointing that rests upon my life?

Single mothers, please know that we must live as anointed vessels before our children as well. We have to handle with care, the anointing that the Lord has given us! Utilize your anointing when it comes to your family! Let the Spirit of God lead you as you minister to your children in the home. Sure, it will bring on warfare like crazy, because the anointing attracts, remember? But be the anointed vessel that the Lord is calling you to be. I have had many encounters of warfare and attacks while trying to teach my children, but I realize it must be instilled in them. When you receive opposition, you're in position! Some people will cause you to believe you're doing too much, as you teach your children gospel, while others will encourage you to keep doing what you're doing. I'm speaking from experience! What MANY don't realize is that as my children are asked to go forth in the house of God, many are shocked at what my children know. As a single mother, the Lord is helping me to lay a foundation for my children. I'm using my anointing to teach!

    I'll never forget a powerful man of God named Evangelist Smith, who spoke over my life when I was just a babe in Christ. He spoke a powerful prophetic word over my life pertaining to a birth that was getting ready to take place, as a woman of God laid hands on my belly. I was such a babe in Christ that I thought to myself, "I'm not pregnant!" I laughed to myself reflecting upon that time. Looking back, the Lord later revealed that ministry was what I was pregnant with in the spirit. The Lord had anointed me for what I now know to be the prophetic ministry. Later, I dreamed that the baby was kicking in my womb. A cousin of mine in the dream expressed to me that there was a baby in my womb. However, I kept denying that the baby was there. I remember her saying to me in the dream, "That's EXACTLY what that is!" Eventually later in other dreams, I dreamed that I was holding the actual baby. POWERFUL!

Learn to thank God for the anointing that's on your life. You may have cried, gone through opposition, difficulties, loneliness, pain, being lied on, talked about and even made fun of. But please know that this is all a part of being chosen, anointed for the Father's use! If they persecuted Jesus, how much more will they persecute you?! Remember, Romans 11:19 declares, "For the gifts and callings of God are without repentance."

You have many who are operating in gifts, yet they haven't repented of their sins and haven't totally surrendered their life to Jesus. So all you have is a gift in operation! Does this mean you won't make mistakes? No! In fact, you will make mistakes and it's a sign of growth needed in those particular areas. However, that does NOT mean stay there!

This by no means gives room for us to condone sin. When the fall is made, REPENT, get back up and keep fighting! What about those that are operating in the anointing for the glory of God that destroys yokes for real? I say to you, hold on to that anointing, nourish it and cherish it! There's such a unique anointing that the Lord has given to the body of Christ and we should be unashamed of what He has anointed us to do. I speak this to myself as well. Anointed mothers, operate in your anointing for HIS GLORY! We are called to win souls and lead them to Christ. Your anointing is attractive all by itself.

CHAPTER 11

Investment (Encouragement to All Mothers)

I would like to talk about investment for a moment. The definition of investment (loyalty, faithfulness, fidelity, dedication, closeness, commitment and attentiveness) is defined as, an act of devoting time, effort, or energy to a particular undertaking with the expectation of a worthwhile result. Out of all the definitions, this particular one captured my attention the most. Just looking at an act of devoting time by itself is intriguing. There's something about time and devotion together. Time is an indefinite continued progress.

With time comes progression and with devotion, comes a WORTHWHILE result. Bear with me, because I'm trying to paint a vivid picture here. What do both of these have in common? Patience! Mothers, whether you're single, married, divorced, or even a widow, think on just how much the Father has invested in us alone. The Lord is someone who has invested His time daily, devoted HIS LIFE and SACRIFICED for you. As we build relationships and intimacy with Him, He's always available! Even when our heart was not there, HIS ALWAYS was!

God took the time to invest in you and me, gifts, talents, a divine plan, and future. Things we can't imagine. Our finite mind can't fathom it all! Jeremiah 29:11 declares, "For I KNOW the thoughts that I think toward YOU, saith the LORD, thoughts of peace, and not of evil, to give YOU an expected end." When I meditate on how much the Lord has invested in me, it's overwhelming! In my private time, I'm brought to tears!

As a single mother, I haven't always walked upright before the Lord, but I'm worth it to Him. "WOW"! For example, I'm reminded of the times when I would be summoned by Jesus to come and commune with Him. He tells me things like, "Come," or "You are being summoned daughter," "Come and commune with me." How He calls me by my name, (Tréasa), shares things with me, loves on me, pours into me and the list goes on! That's to be honored, that's an investment, which equals time!

I don't take it lightly, knowing that I can hear my Father's voice. Sadly MANY people do. Do you know how many people want to hear the voice of God and don't? Or think they have a relationship with Him and it's not considered a relationship to the Father? The Bible declares in Matthew 13:16-17, "But blessed are your eyes, for they see: and your ears, for they hear. For verily I say unto you, That MANY prophets and righteous men have DESIRED to see those things which ye see, and have not seen them; and to hear those things which ye hear, and have not heard them (Don't take it for granted)." Just like the Lord has invested in us, we should invest in Him.

As He has told me before, "I am yours and you are mine!" That's intimacy! Ladies, not even a man can totally satisfy or fulfill the intimacy that I'm referring to here. Over the years, I had to find that out for myself and I'm STILL learning. Yes! I desire to be married one day at the appointed time, but before the Lord can release that man, I must be WHOLE IN HIM and let Him invest in me first! Even when the man of God comes, the Lord will continue to invest, it NEVER ceases! A husband is just the added icing on the cake!

I often think about how the Lord has provided for my three children and I regardless of the circumstances. The favor of God is upon my life, children are blessed, with the hand of God on their lives. Doors have opened, the way has been made, needs have been met and supplied. I believe it was Reverend James Moore, who said it best, "He was there all the time!" Nobody can tell me that the Lord won't invest in someone who's been broken, hurt, used, abused, talked about, rejected, manipulated, taken for granted, and the list goes on. HE WILL STILL INVEST!

Single mothers, hear me: It goes back to our worth! If the Lord is taking the time to invest, what makes us think we should lower the standard for anybody else? God knows our worth and stays devoted to us! That makes YOU the worthwhile result, mentioned earlier!

On the flip side, think about the times you've rejected the Lord's call upon your life because you were attached to this world. In this place, you've put a man in GOD'S PLACE, which is FIRST PLACE, went after your own lusts and desires and forsook HIS WILL for your life. That was me. Maybe it wasn't a man for you, but something had you sold out to IT, instead of YOU being SOLD OUT TO HIM! Still, He called you and made a dedication to HIS INVESTMENT. You my dear, ARE His interest. My God! That's patience, that's unconditional love!

Single mothers, your story may not be similar to mine at all, but be grateful and mindful for what the Lord has invested in you. In order to know this at its FULLEST, we have to seek Jesus for the answers. There's so much to be had of Him! In the world, investors consider several things BEFORE investing in someone and their company. In a nutshell, they want to know what YOU have to offer. They want proof in advance!

In THIS walk of faith, Jesus, as our ultimate investor saw something in us regardless! When we first came to Christ, we came empty handed with nothing in exchange. Think about it...All He wanted was you! He allowed us to come as we were, broken pieces in all. He invested in our shortcomings, falls, heartaches, pains, the bondage, barriers, rebellion, disobedience, selfishness, emptiness, you name it. It was on the list. WHAT AN INVESTOR! I say to you that you have nothing to lose!

To all the mothers around the globe, keep striving, persevere and be all you can be in Christ Jesus! You've overcome some of the greatest obstacles in your life, with the help of the Lord. You're to be honored! Single mothers, remember you're no less than anyone else and you're PRECIOUS in the sight of God. You're more than a conqueror! Romans 8:37 declares, "Nay, in all these things we are more than conquerors through him that loved us." There are times we may feel overlooked or pushed to the side, but believe me, we're NOT! Someone is watching our lifestyle.

Let's humble ourselves under the mighty hand of God and allow HIM to love on us! Dear Heavenly Father, thank You for all the single mothers. Not just them, but every mother in their respective places. I pray that You will impart YOUR wisdom to every SINGLE mother that is raising a child on her own, with the absence of a father. Pour out Your glory upon us and prepare us for the next chapter of our lives, for we need Your strength!

I declare that You're carrying us from a place of pain into a place of joy! For Your Word declares in Psalm 126:5, "They that sow in tears shall reap in joy." I come against guilt and shame in the name of Jesus and I declare Isaiah 61:3 which declares, "To appoint unto them that mourn in Zion, to give unto them beauty for ashes, the oil of joy for mourning, the garment of praise for the spirit of heaviness; that they might be called trees of righteousness, the planting of the LORD, that he might be glorified."

Lord, thank You for the opportunity to share my testimony with many and I declare that whatever we put our hands to do, You will prosper it for Your glory, in Jesus' name! I pray that not only will my testimony uplift and encourage someone, but that YOU will cause change in their lives. I declare growth from these experiences and that I shall bloom in Jesus' name! I pray that the anointing will rest upon this book and that YOU will be glorified through it all! In Jesus' name, Amen!

Isaiah 61:10

I will greatly rejoice in the LORD, my soul shall be joyful in my God; for he hath clothed me with garments of salvation, he hath covered me with the robe of righteousness, as a bridegroom decketh himself with ornaments, and as a bride adorneth herself with her jewels.

About The Author

Prophetess Tréasa Brown was born and raised in Boulder, Colorado. She's the 3rd child of 4 children and was dedicated back to the Lord as a child. Prophetess Brown was raised in the fear and admonition of the Lord and is a God-fearing woman as a result. The Lord saved her in January of 2012, and she was filled with the Holy Ghost, March 28th of 2012. Prophetess Brown was baptized in April of 2016 under Brian Carn Ministries and that same year, baptized by her former Pastor, Superintendent Charles E. Scurles. Prophetess Brown once served as a secretary in the Young Women's Christian Counsel. She was a Primary Sunday School Teacher, Local District Sunshine Band Leader, Bible Band Teacher, Assistant Coordinator, for the Young

Women of Excellence, a Praise and Worship Leader and has preached the Gospel. As a Leader, Prophetess Tréasa Brown is currently serving under the leadership of Pastor Larry Herron and First Lady Herron at Deliverance Jesus Is Coming Ministries. As a woman of God, she loves spending time in the presence of God and she is a prayer warrior and intercessor. Prayer is her passion! Prophetess Brown was destined to be a writer, an author and she has currently written a book by the instruction of Almighty God titled, "Single Mothers and Living for Christ." Also she co-authored a book with Prophetess Kimberly Moses titled, "I Almost Died." She's been a undercover journalist for eight years, writing prophetically while hearing, learning, and studying the voice of God. Prophetess Brown enjoys encouraging others and is drawn to the brokenhearted. The Lord has called her to the nations, the prophetic ministry and to the office of the prophet. Prophetess Brown is yet to be birthed in the healing and deliverance ministry and the Lord is raising her up for His Glory! She has a hunger and a thirst for the things of God and her desire is to please the Father so He will get the Glory out of her life! She's excited about what He is going to do, as her ministry is born. To God Be the Glory!

Index

A

abnormal cells, 36–37
addiction, 24
ambition, 29–30
angels, 51–52, 70
anointed vessels, 72
anointing, 3, 61, 67, 69–75, 83

B

baggage, 33, 53
biopsy, 37
blessing, 5, 36, 57

blood, 3, 5, 29, 34, 38
bondage, 32, 81

C

cervix, 36
change, 10, 26-27, 43, 49-50, 63-64, 82
childish, 20
children, 1, 3, 23-25, 33-34, 40, 43, 52, 58, 65, 68, 72-73, 79, 84
comfort zone, 48
conception, 1-2
Condolences, 4
confirmation, 57-59
conversation, 12

D

damsel, 70
death, 5, 50
deliverance, 14
despair, 28
desperate, 16, 28-29, 31, 65
desperation, 17, 28-31
destiny, 49, 71

disobedience, 37, 81
distractions, 71
divination, 70
dream, 5, 20, 30, 73

E

emotions, 5, 21
emptiness, 26, 81
enemy, 2-5, 9, 16, 71
everlasting, 33
examination, 37
extramarital, 13

F

faith, 1, 47-48, 54, 81
faithfulness, 76
fasting, 57, 60, 66
father, 13, 21, 23-24, 43, 64-65, 69, 74, 77-78, 82, 85
flaws, 41
flesh, 13, 26, 40, 56, 66, 71
foolishness, 51
fornication, 37

G

garments, 82–83
glory, 3, 6, 10, 13, 18, 33, 39–40, 63, 67, 74–75, 82, 85
gospel, 25, 69–70, 73, 85
growth, 2, 9–10, 27, 41, 47–48, 74, 82

H

heal, 13, 16, 33–36, 69
healing, 15–16, 32–34, 36, 39, 85
healing process, 33–35
heart, 10–11, 13, 15, 21, 36, 40–42, 44, 77
heartaches, 28, 81
heat, 34
Holy Ghost, 7, 11–12, 25–26, 50, 56, 63–64, 68, 84
husband, 79

I

identity, 55–56, 59–60, 66
inhabitants, 52

inheritance, 68
intercessor, 37, 85
intimacy, 13, 57, 77, 79
investment, 76, 78, 80

J

Jesus, 10, 13, 22, 25, 29, 31, 34, 36, 42–44, 47–49, 63–64, 66, 68–69, 78, 80–82

K

knowledge, 16, 66

L

LEEP procedure, 37–38
lifestyle, 10, 64, 81
lusts, 12, 66, 80

M

manifestation, 31
ministry, 73, 85
miracle, 1, 3

motherhood, 40

O

opposition, 72, 74

P

pain, 15, 28, 33–35, 74, 81–82
past, 8–10, 18, 48, 54, 62–65
patience, 77, 80
people, 9–10, 27, 30, 39–40, 58, 62, 71–72, 78
pillar, 51–52
position, 11, 29, 33, 72
power, 50, 69
pray, 2, 14, 35, 43, 49, 60, 82
prayer, 14, 16, 39, 42, 57, 66, 70–71, 85
preach, 69
pregnancy, 2
private prayer time, 35
promises, 31, 37, 53
prophetess, 59–60
prophetic, 57, 59
prophetic words, 5, 73
prophets, 2–3, 57–59, 78, 85

R

recklessness, 28
repent, 7, 18, 74
reputation, 63, 66
righteous, 35, 78
righteousness, 35, 82-83

S

salvation, 25, 70, 83
season, 14, 17, 49, 58
selfishness, 81
servants, 53, 70
settling, 29
sexual intercourse, 13
shortcomings, 81
spiritual beings, 56
step, 6, 23, 26, 35, 37, 43, 47, 49, 51
strength, 40-45, 82
stronghold, 12-13

T

Temperance, 13
testify, 13, 63
testimony, 1, 5–7, 35, 38–39, 62, 82
titles, 42, 64–65
tongue, 50
transformation, 10, 32, 63
transparency, 9
trust, 6, 14, 30
truth, 22, 56, 58

U

unhappiness, 28

V

validation, 10, 58
vision, 29–30
voice, 21, 25, 57, 78, 85

W

warfare, 70, 72
weary, 12, 41
witness, 13

worries, 18, 35
worship, 56
wound, 4, 20, 34

www.ingramcontent.com/pod-product-compliance
Lightning Source LLC
Chambersburg PA
CBHW052110110526
44592CB00013B/1557